FirstBass

THE ULTIMATE GUIDE
TO BASS GUITAR FUNDAMENTALS

by Josquin des Pres

Backbeat
Books

San Francisco

Published by Backbeat Books
600 Harrison Street, San Francisco, CA 94107
www.backbeatbooks.com
email: books@musicplayer.com

An imprint of the Music Player Network
Publishers of *Guitar Player*, *Bass Player*, *Keyboard*, *EQ*, and other magazines
United Entertainment Media. Inc.
A CMP Information company

CMP
United Business Media

Distributed to the book trade in the US and Canada by
Publishers Group West, 1700 Fourth Street, Berkeley, CA 94710

Distributed to the music trade in the US and Canada by
Hal Leonard Publishing, P.O. Box 13819, Milwaukee, WI 53213

Cover design and front photo by Paul Haggard
Composition by Chris Ledgerwood

ISBN-13: 978-0-87930-846-9
ISBN-10: 0-87930-846-X

Printed in the United States of America

05 06 07 08 09   5 4 3 2 1

Contents

Introduction

When Leo Fender introduced the first electric bass in 1951, he was responding to requests from musicians for a louder, easier-to-handle instrument. Unlike the acoustic stand-up bass (a.k.a. the bass fiddle, double bass, string bass, contrabass, etc.), Leo's new invention—the Fender Precision Bass—had frets, which allowed bassists to play with more accurate intonation. The "P-Bass" was immediately embraced by thousands of bassists around the world, changing the sound of popular music forever.

First Bass is a step-up guide for the electric bassist, designed to take the beginner to the next level through indispensable fundamentals and exercises. The book covers 50 years of electric bass techniques, concepts, and musical styles. *First Bass* also explores scales, modes, popular-music chord progressions, and bass recording and equipment-buying tips, giving you all the necessary tools to get on with your musical career.

How to Use This Book

The recordings on the included CD should speed up your practicing and help you overcome any difficulties with the book's material. Always practice along with a metronome, drum machine, or drum loops, as this will help you develop a good sense of time and rhythm. Start slowly, and then gradually speed up.

This book is divided into five sections. Don't hesitate to approach the sections in any order you choose; each section is individual and can be used without having worked on the previous sections. However, I strongly recommend you begin your studies with Section 1, Reading Fundamentals. Reading music is important to playing any instrument. Just as being able to read the words of a foreign language helps you pronounce those words, reading music notation will help you understand and interpret the rhythm and notes you are playing.

Also important is Section 5, Bass Playing Styles. The best way to find your own signature sound is to play a wide variety of musical styles. Also, being versatile will often lead to employment—in other words, you'll get more gigs.

Getting the Right Gear

Choosing the bass guitar that's right for you

When you start to play bass, one of the most important things to do is to choose the right instrument. Beginner musicians usually choose an instrument similar to the one used by the player they look up to and who has most influenced them. When I first started playing bass back in the late '60s, there were pretty much only three brands to choose from: Fender, Gibson, and Rickenbacker. Today, there are literally hundreds of brands of bass guitars. Luckily, most of them are very good, including many inexpensive instruments manufactured in Asia and Latin America. Most companies have figured out how to inexpensively build great instruments.

However, there are a few rules to follow. Pick an instrument that feels good in your hands, and make sure you try it on with a strap. It's very important that you choose a well-balanced instrument. If your bass is neck-heavy, you will find yourself constantly pulling up the neck and re-positioning the instrument, and you will probably experience arm and shoulder pain after extended playing periods. Choose an instrument with two pickups and, if possible, electronics with both passive and active options. This will allow you a wider variety of sounds. Also, keep in mind that the heavier the instrument, the denser the wood. Since it is harder for a string to resonate and vibrate through dense wood, lighter woods such as alder and poplar will give you a deeper tone, while heavier woods like maple will give you a thinner tone.

Choosing the bass amp that's right for you

One of my first recommendations is that you choose an amp powerful enough to practice and to play gigs. If you're looking for an affordable high-power amp that can handle road abuse, a solid-state amp is probably the right choice. Tube amps are costlier and more fragile. The main difference is in the way a tube amp overdrives compared to a solid-state amp: Tube distortion and overdrive sounds warmer in comparison to solid-state distortion.

Also, decide whether you want a combo amp (speaker and amp in the same box) or a separate amp head and cabinet. Combos are, of course, easier to carry, and most of today's combo amps are very well designed and powerful enough for most venues. In addition, many combo amps allow to you add an extra cabinet to reinforce the low end, in case you need it for a larger venue.

Today's properly built 4x10 speaker cabinet designs are very good at reproducing low frequencies—even those from a 5-string's lowest notes. (The term "4x10" means they have four 10" speakers.) Cabinets with a 15" speaker can move a room with lots of low-end rumble, but these speakers are a bit less accurate in the high midrange. Although very few manufacturers make them, in my opinion the ideal cabinet has a 15" speaker and two 8" or two 10" speakers in one enclosure. This combination provides the best of both worlds.

Choosing the right strings for your playing style

The strings on your bass are the source of your sound. Choosing the right strings for your playing style will help shape and define your sound.

Roundwound strings: This is the most popular type of strings. Pioneered by Rotosound, roundwound strings were first introduced in the mid '60s and used by the Who's John Entwistle, Chris Squire of Yes, Led Zeppelin's John Paul Jones, and many others.

Roundwound strings instantly changed the instrument's sound, giving the notes more definition and bringing the instrument to the forefront of rock & roll. Roundwound strings are ideal for slapping, tapping, and fingerstyle playing. If you are a soloist, these are definitely the strings for you.

Flatwound strings: The first Fender basses came equipped with flatwound strings to more closely replicate the sound of an upright "doghouse" bass. Today, flatwound strings still give that fat, warm sound you need for Old School jazz, country, and R&B. James Jamerson helped shape the Motown sound with flatwound strings.

Phosphor bronze strings: With the growing emergence of acoustic bass guitars, string companies have felt the need to create a string especially designed for these acoustic instruments. Similar to the bronze strings made for acoustic guitar, phosphor bronze strings have a slightly looser feel than the regular stainless-steel-core strings, and they give you brilliance, clarity, and deep, rich bass.

Black nylon strings: Most famously heard on the Beatles' *Abbey Road*, black nylon strings provide a super-smooth sound like that of flatwound strings, but with a more hollow tone. They are ideal on fretless acoustic basses and will help give your electric instrument a jazzy upright-bass sound.

Effects for the bass guitar

Although many bassists have used distortion, overdrive, reverb, and delay, the most commonly used effects for the bass guitar are compression and chorus. Compression can help even out the levels of your bass performances, especially if you are a slapper. If you use a solid-state amplifier, a good compressor can also help emulate a tube bass amp's warmth. Chorus can also be a nice addition to your effects arsenal; it can make your sound fuller, especially with a fretless instrument. Another great-sounding effect for bass is the auto-wah (a.k.a. envelope filter). If you are a slapper, you will love the auto-wah's funky sounds and aggressive response. In general, the best way to find effects that are right for your playing style is to try them. Numerous companies have developed high-quality, inexpensive multi-effect signal processors containing the most popular effects.

A few recording tips

With the ever-growing popularity of recording software and inexpensive digital recording equipment, it's important to address recording the bass. If you own recording software and the proper interface to record an analog instrument into your computer, you have a serious practicing and recording tool on your hands. There is an abundance of drum loop CDs on the market. By assembling these loops, you will be able to prepare drum tracks and music beds that are ideal for practicing, developing new songs, and preparing yourself to perform with real players.

There are two ways of recording an electric bass: either by taking a direct feed from the instrument and running it through a direct box, or by plugging into an amp and miking a speaker cabinet. In both professional and home studios, most bass recording is done direct. This approach solves a lot of sound-leakage problems and makes it easier to get a nice, clean sound. A common practice is to "warm up" a direct-recorded signal by re-running it through a bass amp and miking the amp's speaker. Today there are also software plug-ins that can re-create a miked bass amplifier's warm, fat sound.

When recording an acoustic bass guitar, experiment with going direct and miking the bass at the same time. Done properly, combining both signals will give you a fat acoustic sound similar to that of an upright bass.

Proper Fretting- and Plucking-Hand Playing Positions

Fretting-hand position

Fretting-hand position

Plucking-hand position

Notational Symbols

Backbeat Books uses the following symbols to indicate fingerings and techniques.

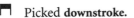

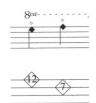

Slide (capital S): If the notes are tied, pluck only the first. When there is no tie, pluck both notes.

Harmonics are indicated by tiny circles over the note heads, which indicate actual pitch; the tablature shows where the harmonic is played.

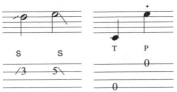

A slide symbol before or after a single note indicates a slide to or from an unspecific pitch.

A **thumb slap** is indicated with a capital T; a **pop** by a capital P.

Capital B indicates a **bend**, either from a grace-note or a note with a full duration value.

Capital R indicates a **release**: Pre-bend to the note in parentheses, play, and then release the bend to the indicated note.

Capital H indicates a **hammer-on**.

Capital PO indicates a **pull-off**.

Finger vibrato.

Trill.

Picked **downstroke**.

Picked **upstroke**.

4 ● **Fretting-hand fingerings** are indicated by numerals. (1=index finger, 2=middle finger, etc.).

How Tablature Works.
The horizontal lines represent the bass strings, the bottom line being *E* and the top being *G*. Numbers designate the frets (0 indicates an open string). For instance, a 2 positioned on the bottom line would mean play the 2nd fret on the *E* string. Time values are shown in the standard notation directly above the tablature. Special symbols and instructions appear between the notation and tablature staves.

Section 1
Reading Fundamentals

A few important rules to follow every time you practice:

- When practicing, always use a metronome or rhythm device (drum machine, drum loops, etc.).

- Start each exercise slowly, somewhere between 60 and 80 beats per minute (bpm) depending on the difficulty of the exercise.

- Always sing or hum along with every note you play. This will help you develop your ear. Good reading skills and ear training go hand in hand.

- The accompanying CD will help you understand the exercises—use it! In this book, the CD track number appears next to each recorded example.

- Read groups of notes as if you were reading words. Avoid the outdated "spelling" method of reading rhythms (i.e., "one e and a, two e and a, three e and a, four e and a"). Instead, think as follows:

= taa taa

= taa ta ta

= ta ta taa

= ta taa ta

This method will have you reading rhythms much faster.

Staff & clef
A music staff has five lines and four spaces. Bass music is written in the bass clef.

Bass clef

Measures & bar lines

Measures divide the music into small sections. Bar lines separate the measures. The end of a large section (verse, chorus, bridge, etc.) is marked by a double bar.

Time signatures

The most common time signature in popular music is 4/4. In this case, the top number indicates there are four beats per measure, while the bottom number indicates that each quarter-note gets one count. In other words, "4/4" means there are four quarter-notes per measure.

Note duration

The shape of a note indicates its duration. Some notes are hollow, some have stems, and some have stems and flags.

Consecutive eighth-notes are connected by their flags to make them easier to read.

Consecutive 16th-notes are connected by their flags to make them easier to read

Rests

Each type of note has a silent equivalent called a rest. Do not play for the duration of a rest.

whole-rest	half-rest	quarter-rest	eighth-rest	sixteenth-rest
(4 beats)	(2 beats)	(1 beat)	(1/2 beat)	(1/4 beat)

Pitch

The vertical position of a note on the staff indicates its pitch. The higher the pitch, the higher a note's position on the staff. Ledger lines are used to expand the staff's range.

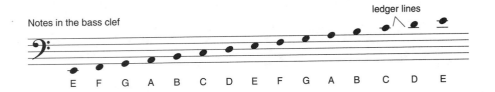

Reading studies with rhythms only

Practice the following examples with a metronome.

Tap your foot down on each beat:

Each beat (one metronome click or one foot tap) equals one quarter-note.

Bring your foot up on each offbeat.

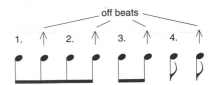

Play each of the following examples on a single *D* note, the 5th fret on the *A* string.

Ex. 1: Combining whole-notes and half-notes

Ex. 2: Combining whole-notes, half-notes, and quarter-notes

Ex. 3: Combining whole-notes, half-notes, quarter-notes, and eighth-notes

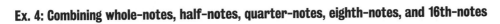

Ex. 4: Combining whole-notes, half-notes, quarter-notes, eighth-notes, and 16th-notes

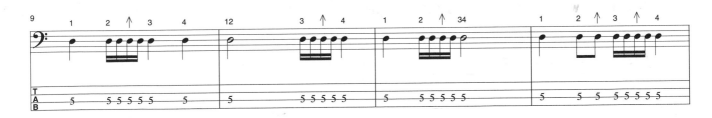

Ex. 5: Combining whole-notes, half-notes, quarter-notes, whole-rests, half-rests, and quarter-rests

ON
5
TRACK

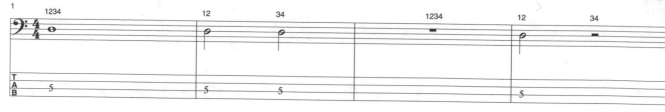

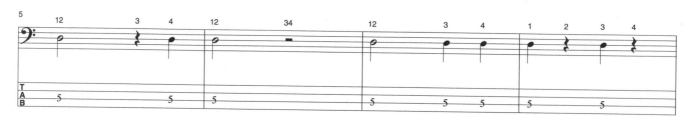

Ex. 6: Combining half-notes, quarter-notes, eighth-notes, half-rests, and quarter-rests

ON
6
TRACK

Ex. 7: Combining half-notes, quarter-notes, eighth-notes, quarter-rests, and eighth-rests

Ex. 8: Eighth- and 16th-note combinations

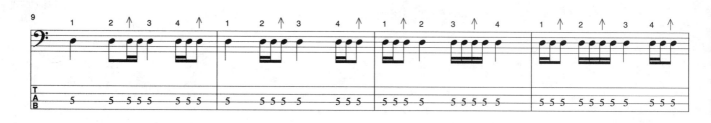

Ex. 9: More eighth- and 16th-note combinations

Ex. 10: Adding eighth-rests

ON
10
TRACK

Ex. 11: More adding eighth-rests

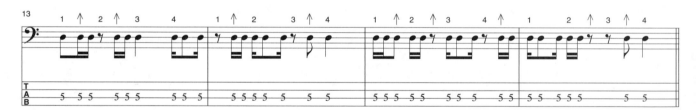

Ex. 12: Adding 16th-rests

The dot

A dot added to a note or a rest increases its value by half.

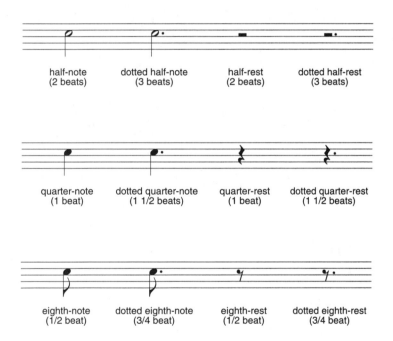

half-note
(2 beats)

dotted half-note
(3 beats)

half-rest
(2 beats)

dotted half-rest
(3 beats)

quarter-note
(1 beat)

dotted quarter-note
(1 1/2 beats)

quarter-rest
(1 beat)

dotted quarter-rest
(1 1/2 beats)

eighth-note
(1/2 beat)

dotted eighth-note
(3/4 beat)

eighth-rest
(1/2 beat)

dotted eighth-rest
(3/4 beat)

Ex. 13: Dotted half-notes and dotted quarter-notes

Ex. 14: Dotted half-notes and dotted quarter-notes with rests

Sometimes you'll see a note with two dots, or a double-dotted note. The second dot extends the note's duration by an additional one-fourth, so the two dots together extend the note's duration by a total of three-quarters. Therefore, a double-dotted half-note lasts for seven eighth-notes, a double-dotted quarter-note lasts for seven 16th-notes, etc.

The tie

A tie extends a note's duration into the next note it is tied to. Ties are also used to extend notes over the bar line into the next measure.

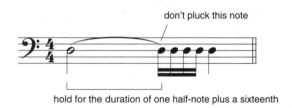

don't pluck this note

hold for the duration of one half-note plus a sixteenth

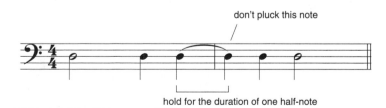

don't pluck this note

hold for the duration of one half-note

Ex. 15: Tied half-notes, quarter-notes, eighth-notes, and 16th-notes

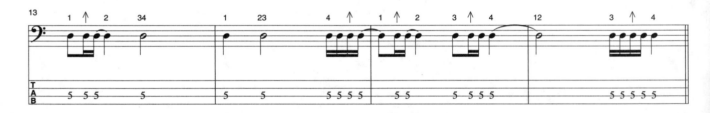

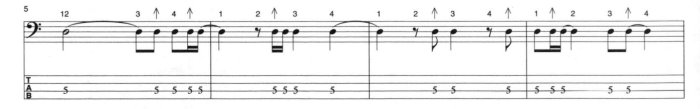

Ex. 16: Tied half-notes, quarter-notes, eighth-notes, and 16th-notes with rests

Ex. 17: Dotted and tied notes with rests

Ex. 18: More dotted and tied notes with rests

The triplet

A triplet is a group of three notes or rests performed in the time normally taken by just two notes or rests of the same value.

A quarter-note triplet is a series of three quarter-notes (or rests) of equal value that occur inside a half-note group:

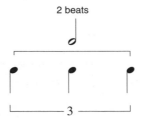

An eighth-note triplet is a series of three eighth-notes (or rests) of equal value that occur inside a quarter-note group:

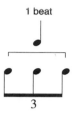

A 16th-note triplet is a series of three 16th-notes (or rests) of equal value that occur inside an eighth-note group:

Ex. 19: Quarter-note and half-note triplets

Ex. 20: 16th-note triplets

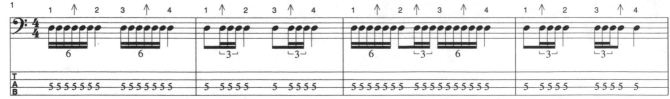

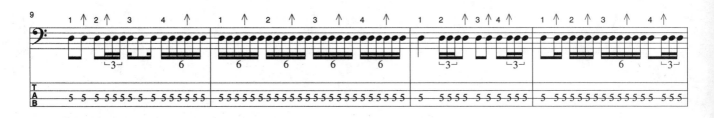

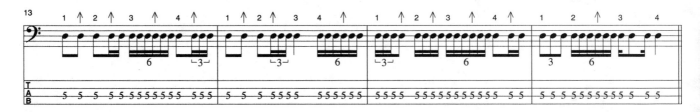

Ex. 21: Triplets with rests

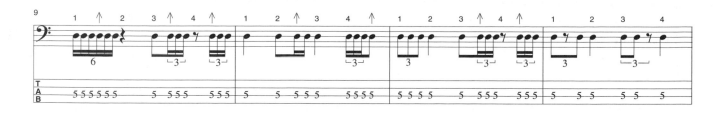

Ex. 22: Recapitulation of all previous rhythmic patterns

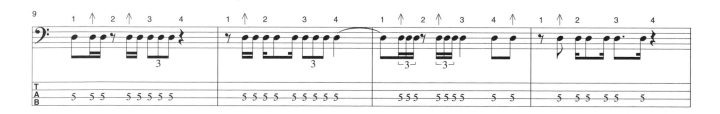

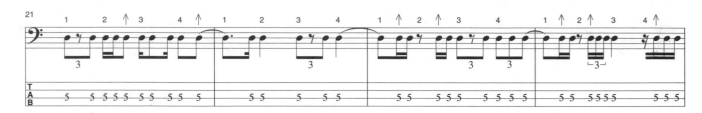

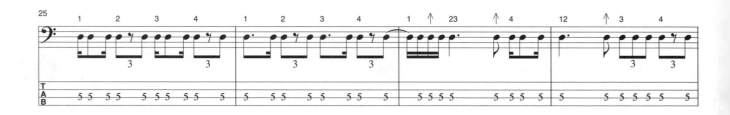

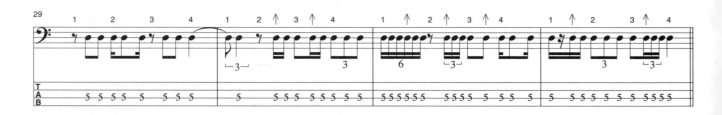

Ex. 23: More recapitulation of all previous rhythmic patterns

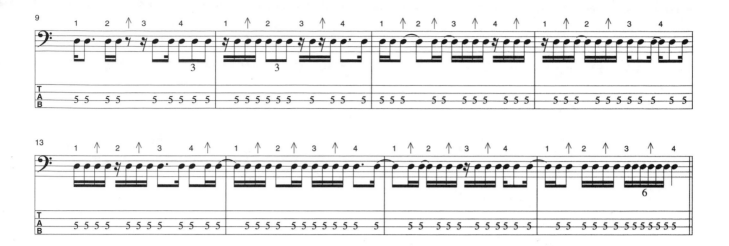

The notes on the bass guitar neck

(For an explanation of enharmonic pitches such as *G♯/A♭*, see page 41.)

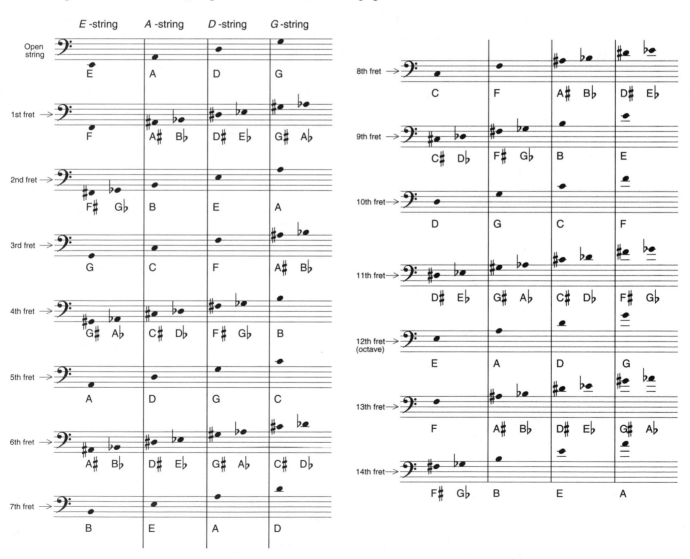

The notes on the neck, one string at a time.

Notes on the *E* string:

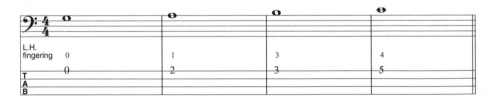

Notes on the *A* string:

Notes on the *D* string:

Notes on the *G* string:

Ex. 24: Rhythms and notes on the E string

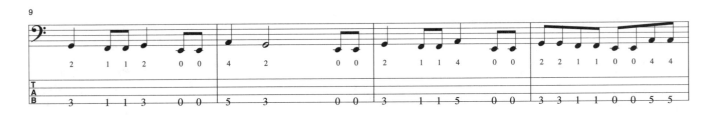

Ex. 25: Rhythms and notes on the E and A strings

Ex. 26: Rhythms and notes on the *E*, *A*, and *D* strings

Ex. 27: Rhythms and notes on the E, A, D, and G strings

Ex. 28: Reading studies on all four strings without fretting-hand fingering

In the following exercises, I have purposely omitted bass guitar tablature. This is to help you focus on reading music notation only. Use tablature only if needed.

Ex. 29: Reading studies on all four strings without fretting-hand fingering or tablature

Ex. 30: More reading studies on all four strings without fretting-hand fingering or tablature

Accidentals

An accidental is a sign used to raise or lower a note by one half-step.

Sharp (#)

The sharp sign raises a note by one half-step.

Flat (♭)

The flat sign lowers a note by one half-step.

Natural (♮)

The natural sign cancels a previous sharp or flat.

Accidentals remain in force for the whole measure in which they appear, unless they are cancelled by a natural. Naturals are sometimes used in the measure immediately following an accidental as a reminder that the sharp or flat is no longer in effect.

Ex. 31: Whole-notes with sharps and flats

ON TRACK 31

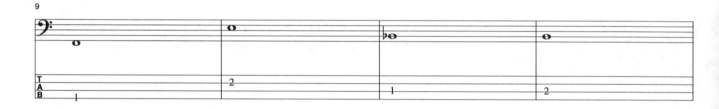

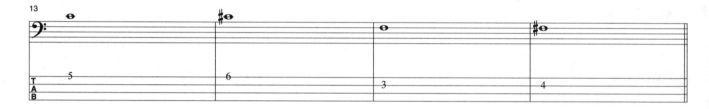

Ex. 32: Half-notes with sharps and flats

ON TRACK 32

Ex. 33: Half-notes with sharps, flats, and naturals

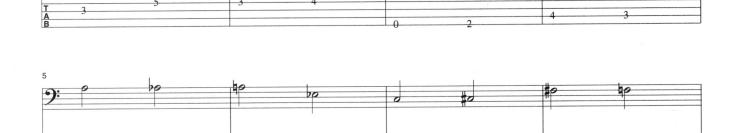

Ex. 34: Whole-notes, half-notes, quarter-notes, and eighth-notes with sharps, flats, and naturals

Enharmonic equivalents

When two note names refer to the same pitch (e.g., G♯ and A♭), they are called enharmonic equivalents. Most music pieces use only one of these notes—either the sharp or flat version. However, the following exercise uses both to help you recognize enharmonic equivalents and learn how to read the same pitch in two ways.

Ex. 35

Scales & Key Signatures

Major scales

C major scale

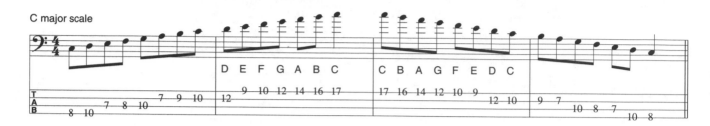

G major scale

D major scale

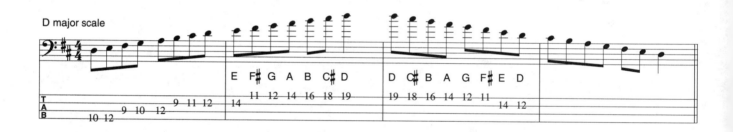

A major scale

E major scale

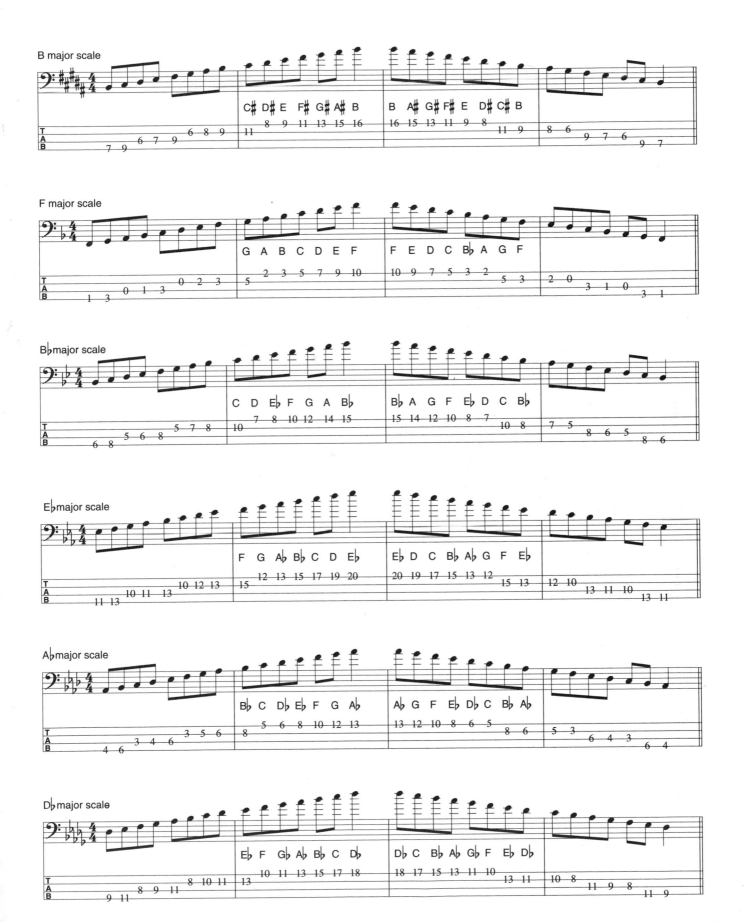

Minor scales

A minor scale

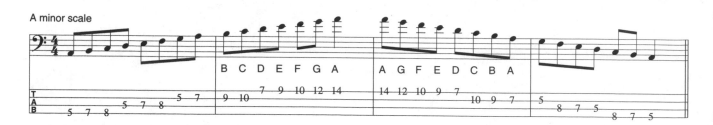

E minor scale

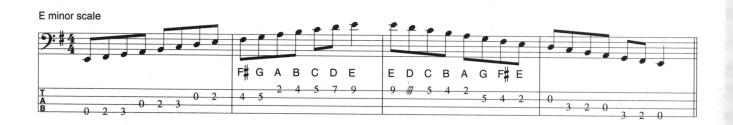

B minor scale

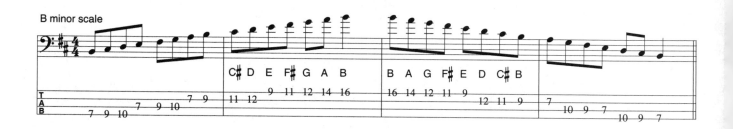

F♯ minor scale

C♯ minor scale

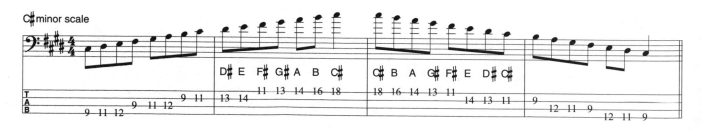

The major key signatures most commonly used in popular music are: C major, G major, D major, A major, and E major.

Ex. 36: C major (no flats or sharps)

Ex. 37: G major (one sharp: F♯)

Ex. 38: D major (two sharps: F♯, C♯)

Ex. 39: A major (three sharps: F#, C#, G#)

Ex. 40: E major (four sharps: F#, C#, G#, D#)

The minor key signatures most commonly used in popular music are: A minor, E minor, B minor, D minor, and G minor.

Ex. 41: A minor (no flats or sharps)

Ex. 42: E minor (one sharp: F♯)

Ex. 43: B minor (two sharps: F#, C#)

Ex. 44: D minor (one flat: B♭)

Ex. 45: G minor (two flats: B♭, E♭)

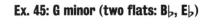

Section 2
Warmup & Dexterity Exercises

Fretting–Hand Warm-up & Dexterity Exercises

Ex. 1 (Play twice, and then move up in half-steps)

Ex. 2 (Play twice, and then move up in half-steps)

Ex. 3 (Play twice, and then move up in half-steps)

Ex. 4 (Play twice, and then move up in half-steps)

Ex. 5 (Play twice, and then move up in half-steps)

Plucking-Hand Warmup & Dexterity Exercises

Ex. 6

R.H. fingering: 1 2 1 2 1 2 1 2 1 2 1 2 1 2 1 2   1 2 1 2 1 2 1 2 1 2 1 2   1 2 1 2 1 2 1 2 1 2 1 2   1 2 1 2 1 2 1 2 1 2 1 2

TAB: 3 3 3 3 3 3 3 3 3 3 3 3 3 3 3 3   3 3 3 3 3 3 3 3 3 3 3 3   3 3 3 3 3 3 3 3 3 3 3 3   3 3 3 3 3 3 3 3 3 3 3 3

Ex. 7

R.H. fingering: 2 1 2 1 2 1 2 1 2 1 2 1 2 1   2 1 2 1 2 1 2 1 2 1 2 1   2 1 2 1 2 1 2 1 2 1 2 1   2 1 2 1 2 1 2 1 2 1 2 1

TAB: 3 3 3 3 3 3 3 3 3 3 3 3 3 3 3   3 3 3 3 3 3 3 3 3 3 3 3   3 3 3 3 3 3 3 3 3 3 3 3   3 3 3 3 3 3 3 3 3 3 3 3

Ex. 8

R.H. fingering: 1 2 1 1 2 1 2 2 1 2 1 1 2 1 2 2   1 2 1 1 2 1 2 2 1 2 1 1 2 1 2 2   1 2 1 1 2 1 2 2 1 2 1 1 2 1 2 2   1 2 1 1 2 1 2 2 1 2 1 1 2 1 2 2

TAB: 3 3 3 3 3 3 3 3 3 3 3 3 3 3 3 3   3 3 3 3 3 3 3 3 3 3 3 3   3 3 3 3 3 3 3 3 3 3 3 3   3 3 3 3 3 3 3 3 3 3 3 3

Ex. 9

R.H. fingering: 1 1 2 1 2 2 1 2 1 1 2 1 2 2 1 2   1 1 2 1 2 1 2 2 1 1 2 1 2 2   1 1 2 1 2 1 2 2 1 1 2 1 2 2   1 1 2 1 2 1 2 2 1 1 2 1 2 2

TAB: 3 3 3 3 3 3 3 3 3 3 3 3 3 3 3 3   3 3 3 3 3 3 3 3 3 3 3 3   3 3 3 3 3 3 3 3 3 3 3 3   3 3 3 3 3 3 3 3 3 3 3 3

Ex. 10 (Note that when you're descending, the plucking-hand fingerings reverse.)

R.H.
fingering: 1 2 1 2 1 2 1 2 1 2 1 2 1 2 1 2   1 2 1 2 2 1 2 1 1 2 1 2 2 1 2 1   1 2 1 2 1 2 1 2 1 2 1 2 1 2 1 2   1 2 1 2 2 1 2 1 1 2 1 2 2 1 2 1

Ex. 11 (Note that when you're descending, the plucking-hand fingerings reverse.)

R.H.
fingering: 2 1 2 1 2 1 2 1 2 1 2 1 2 1 2 1   2 1 2 1 1 2 1 2 2 1 2 1 1 2 1 2   1 2 1 2 1 2 1 2 1 2 1 2 1 2 1 2   2 1 2 1 1 2 1 2 2 1 2 1 1 2 1 2

Ex. 12 (Note that when you're descending, the plucking-hand fingerings *do not* reverse.)

R.H.
fingering: 1 2 1 1 2 1 2 2 1 2 1 1 2 1 2 2   1 2 1 1 1 2 1 1 1 2 1 1 1 2 1 1   1 2 1 2 1 2 1 2 1 2 1 2 1 2 1 2   1 2 1 1 1 2 1 1 1 2 1 1 1 2 1 1

Ex. 13 (Note that when you're descending, the plucking-hand fingerings *do not* reverse.)

R.H.
fingering: 2 1 2 2 1 2 1 1 2 1 2 2 1 2 1 1   2 1 2 2 2 1 2 2 2 1 2 2 2 1 2 2   2 1 2 2 1 2 1 1 2 1 2 2 1 2 1 1   2 1 2 2 2 1 2 2 2 1 2 2 2 1 2 2

Fretting- & Plucking-Hand Synchronization Exercises

Ex. 14: Using 4th and 5th intervals (Note that when you're descending, the plucking-hand fingerings *do not* reverse.)

Ex. 15: Using 4th and 5th intervals, alternate fingering (Note that when you're descending, the plucking-hand fingerings *do not* reverse.)

Ex. 16: Using octave intervals

Ex. 17: Using inverted octave intervals

Section 3
How to Build Solid Bass Lines

Walking Bass Lines

A walking bass line is one consisting mostly (or entirely) of quarter-notes, with few or no rests. Although walking bass lines are commonly used in jazz and blues, practicing walking bass is a quick, effective way to learn how to build harmonically solid musical phrases in any style. The fact that you don't have to worry about various rhythmic patterns makes it especially easy.

In the following exercises, we are going to focus on quarter-note patterns played with common intervals (root, 3rd, 5th, octave, etc). Each four-note pattern leads into the next chord by using a leading note (or passing note). A leading note is usually a half-step above or below the next root.

Make sure you listen to the audio on the provided CD to understand the exact feel of these exercises.

Note: On the audio tracks for this section, I've removed the bass line from the second half of each track, so that you can practice the line along with the rest of the band.

Chord progression No. 1

Ex. 1: Root–5th–root–leading note

Ex. 2: Root–5th–octave–leading note

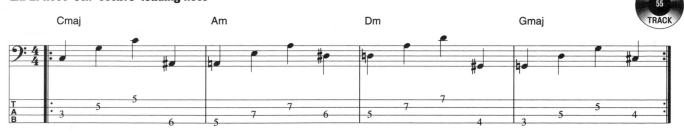

Ex. 3: Octave–5th–root–leading note

Ex. 4: Root–3rd–5th–leading note

Ex. 5: Combining all previous patterns

Chord progression No. 2

Ex. 6: Root–5th–root–leading note

ON TRACK 59

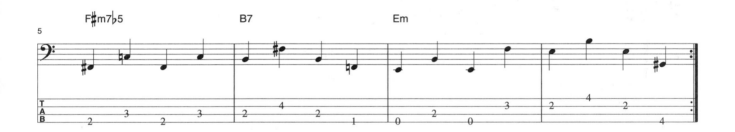

Ex. 7: Root–5th–octave–leading note

ON TRACK 60

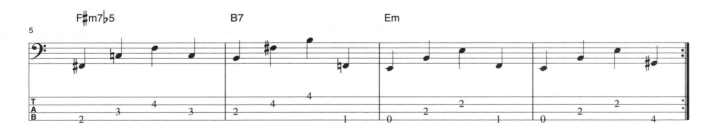

Ex. 8: Octave–5th–root–leading note

ON TRACK 61

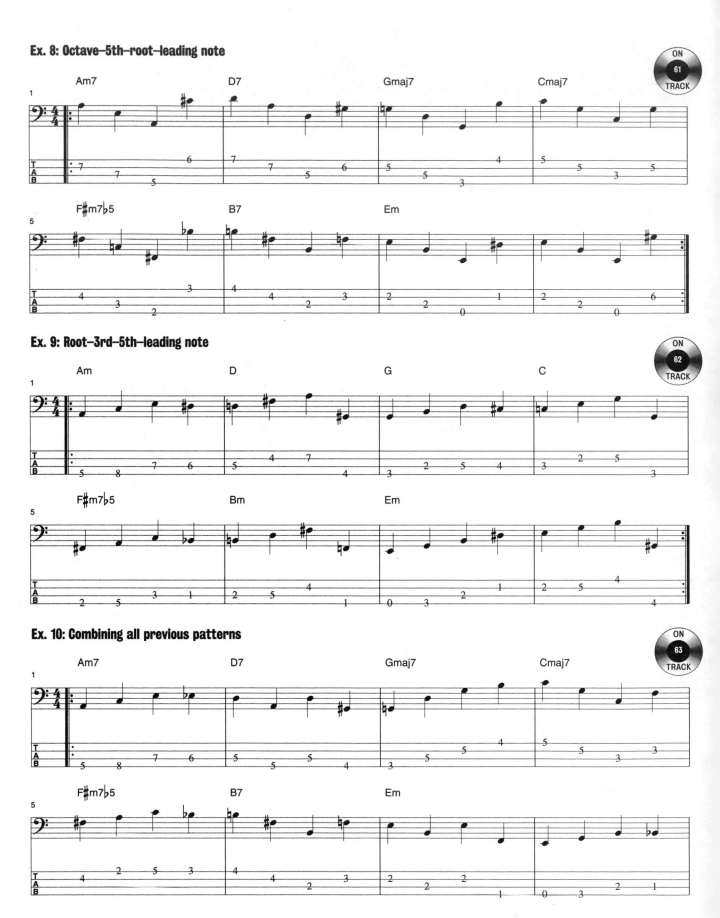

Ex. 9: Root–3rd–5th–leading note

ON TRACK 62

Ex. 10: Combining all previous patterns

ON TRACK 63

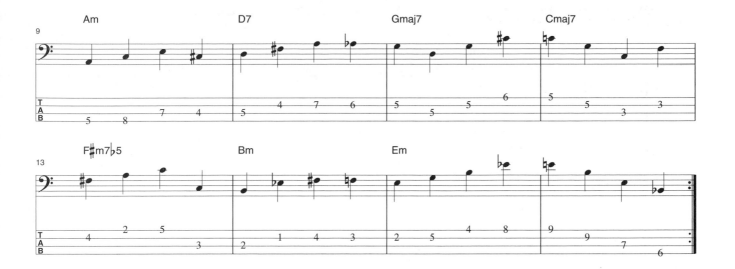

Creating Bass Fills: Modes & Scales

The key to creating solid and harmonically sound bass fills and solos is to know your modes. Let's look at the modes most commonly used in popular music, and their corresponding chords.

Although all the following examples are in the key of C, they are moveable to all key signatures.

In the key of C:

Ex. 11: Ionian mode (for chords Cm, C9, C6, C6/9, Cm7, Cm7/9)

Ex. 12: Dorian mode (for chords Dm, Dm9, Dm7, Dm7/9, Dm11)

Ex. 13: Phrygian mode (for chords Em, Em♭9)

Phrygian

Ex. 14: Lydian mode (for chords Fm7♭5, Fm7♭5/9, Fm7#11)

Lydian

Ex. 15: Mixolydian mode (for chords G7, G7/9, Gsus4, G7sus4, G11, G9/6, G13)

Mixolydian

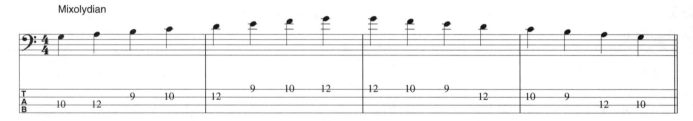

Ex. 16: Aeolian mode (for chords Am, Am9, Am7, Am7/9, Am11, Am11/9)

Aeolian

Ex. 17: Locrian mode (for chords Bm7♭5, a.k.a. B half-diminished)

Locrian

Diminished scale in C (a.k.a. symmetric scale)

Ex. 18

Augmented scale in C (a.k.a. whole-tone scale)

Ex. 19

Practicing modes over various chord progressions

In order to help you learn your modes inside and out, I have developed an exercise called tetrachord inversions. A tetrachord is a series of four consecutive notes making up an interval of a 4th. For example: In the *C* major scale, *C–D–E–F* is the first tetrachord, and *G–A–B–C* is the second tetrachord. Practicing the following tetrachord inversion exercises will help you learn your modes, so you'll be able to create great bass fills without sounding like you are practicing up and down a scale.

Once you get through the following exercises, do the same patterns over just about any chord progressions you can get your hands on. (Make sure you listen to the audio on the provided CD to understand the exact feel of these exercises.)

Chord progression No. 1

Ex. 20

ON TRACK 64

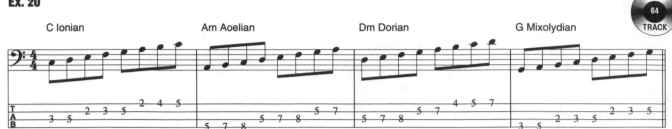

Ex. 21: Inverting tetrachords (1st tetrachord up, 2nd tetrachord down)

ON TRACK 65

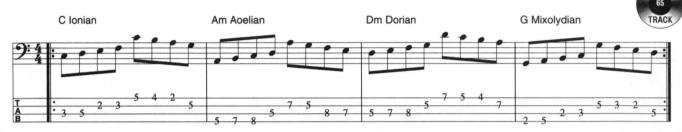

Ex. 22: Inverting tetrachords (2nd tetrachord down, 1st tetrachord up)

ON TRACK 66

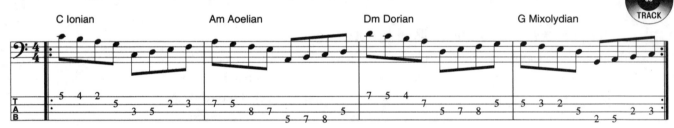

Ex. 23: Inverting tetrachords (1st tetrachord down, 2nd tetrachord up)

ON TRACK 67

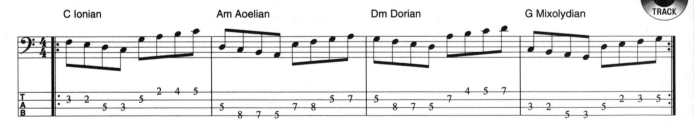

Ex. 24: Inverting tetrachords (2nd tetrachord up, 1st tetrachord down)

ON TRACK 68

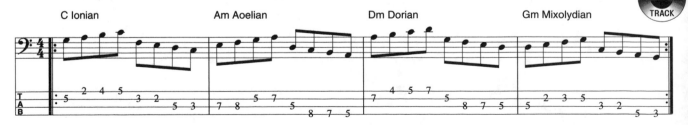

Chord progression No. 2

Ex. 25

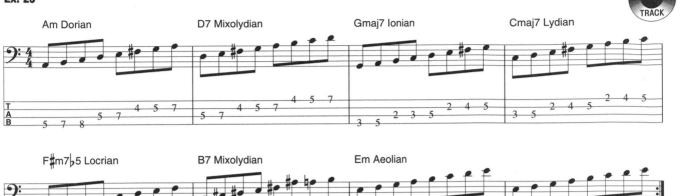

Am Dorian — D7 Mixolydian — Gmaj7 Ionian — Cmaj7 Lydian

F#m7♭5 Locrian — B7 Mixolydian — Em Aeolian

Ex. 26: Inverting tetrachords (1st tetrachord up, 2nd tetrachord down)

Am Dorian — D7 Mixolydian — Gmaj7 Ionian — Cmaj7#11 Lydian

F#m7♭5 — B7 Mixolydian — Em Aeolian

Ex. 27: Inverting tetrachords (2nd tetrachord down, 1st tetrachord up)

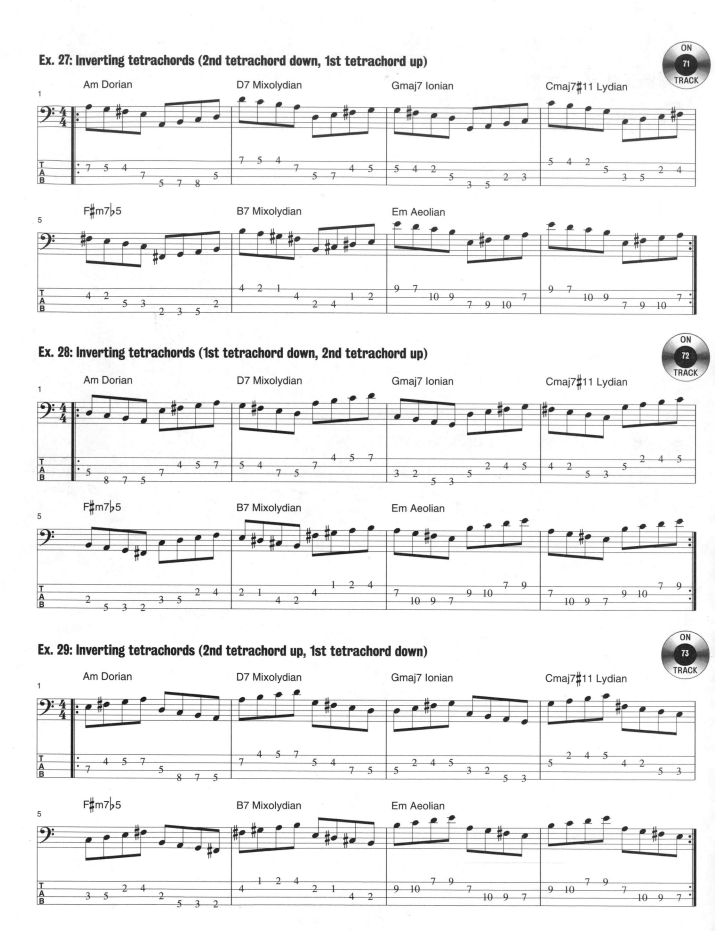

Ex. 28: Inverting tetrachords (1st tetrachord down, 2nd tetrachord up)

Ex. 29: Inverting tetrachords (2nd tetrachord up, 1st tetrachord down)

Section 4
Techniques & Concepts

String Muting

String muting is one of the most useful techniques to develop a great groove. String muting can be compared to the hi-hat hits in between the kick and snare in a drum groove: They link the two together. Some of the greatest bass players of all time have used string muting as part of their distinctive sound; they include James Jamerson (Motown), John Paul Jones (Led Zeppelin), Flea (Red Hot Chili Peppers), Rocco Prestia (Tower Of Power), Bunny Brunel, Victor Wooten, Steve Bailey, and many more.

String muting

Here's how it works: Fret a *C* note, and then pluck it with your other hand. The result is a clear, sustained note. Now release your fretting-hand finger pressure just enough so that the string no longer touches the fret, and pluck the string again. This time, the result should be a hollow, thud-like sound.

Practice the following exercises to develop a good string-muting technique. The first time through each exercise, use the top row of plucking-hand fingerings; then use the bottom row. Be patient—at first this can seem boring, but once you know how to do it, it can turn into a lot of fun.

Make sure you listen to the audio on the provided CD to understand the exact feel of these exercises.

Ex. 1

Ex. 2

ON 75 TRACK

Ex. 3

ON 76 TRACK

Ex. 4

ON 77 TRACK

Ex. 5

ON 78 TRACK

Ex. 6

ON 79 TRACK

Ex. 7

Ex. 8

String Raking

String raking involves playing a succession of muted notes that descend across several strings, usually ending with a regular sustained note.

As before, use the top row of plucking-hand fingerings first, and then use the bottom row when you repeat. Make sure you listen to the audio on the provided CD to understand the exact feel of these exercises.

String raking

Ex. 9

Ex. 10 (same as Ex. 9 but with alternate fingering)

ON 82 TRACK

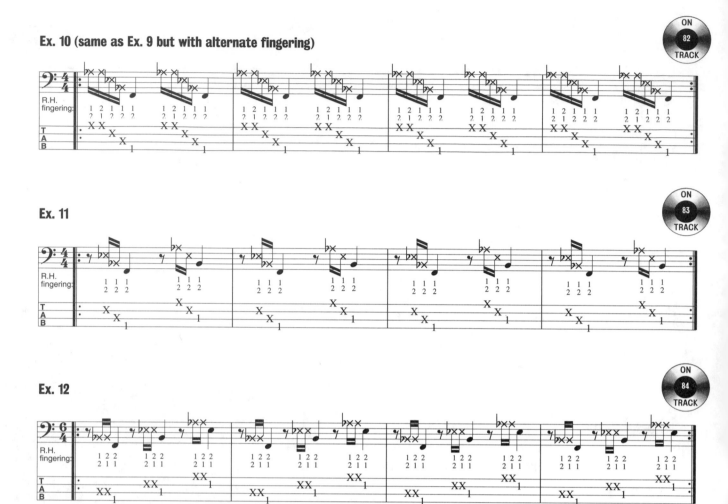

Ex. 11

ON 83 TRACK

Ex. 12

ON 84 TRACK

Riffs Using String Muting & String Raking

Note: In some of these Examples, you'll see slanted lines before or after certain notes. These are slides (also indicated in the notation with an "S")—while keeping a fretting-hand finger depressed all the way, pluck the string and then quickly slide your finger up or down to the proper fret. If a slide marking follows a note or connects two notes, sound the note and then keep your fretting-hand finger depressed while you slide up or down the string to the next note.

ON 85 TRACK

Ex. 13

Ex. 14

ON 86 TRACK

Ex. 15

ON 87 TRACK

Ex. 16

ON 88 TRACK

Slap Bass

The slap-bass technique was pioneered on electric bass in the late '60s by Sly & the Family Stone's Larry Graham. Some people associate slap bass only with funk music, but today this popular technique appears in a wide variety of styles.

Here are the components of slap-bass technique, along with bass patterns that put them to use.

Thumb slap (T)

Slap the string with the side of the plucking-hand thumb.

Thumb Slap

Ex. 17

Ex. 18: Bass riff using the thumb slap technique. Notice the wavy line over the *F* at the end of bar 2: It's a vibrato marking, which tells you to give the note a little shake, to create a rapid fluctuation in pitch.

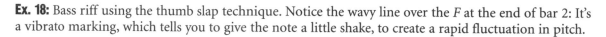

Index-finger pop

Index-finger pop (P)

Pull the string with the plucking-hand index finger and release it so that it rebounds against the fingerboard.

Ex. 19

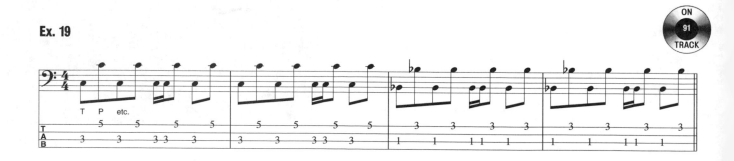

Ex. 19 *continued*

ON
92
TRACK

Ex. 20: Bass riff using the thumb slap and the index-finger pop techniques. In this Example, notice the tie-like markings that connect notes with different pitches. These are called slurs, and they indicate that you don't pluck the second note, but instead sound it with the fretting hand.

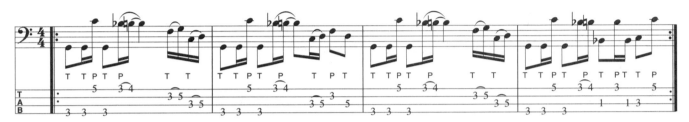

If a note is connected to a higher note with a slur, it means you usually sound the second note with a hammer-on technique (indicated in the notation with an "H"): Without plucking, quickly and firmly fret the second note so that the string continues to vibrate at the higher pitch.

If a note is connected to a lower note with a slur, it means you usually sound the second note with a pull-off technique (indicated in the notation with a "PO"), in which you actually pluck the note with your fretting hand. Instead of merely lifting your fretting-hand finger, give the string a little pluck, so that the string vibrates at the lower pitch.

Muted slap (MS) & muted pop (MP)

These are similar to the thumb slap and index-finger pop techniques, but you execute them while muting the strings with your fretting hand.

Muted slap and muted pop

Bass riffs using the muted slap and the muted pop techniques.

Ex. 21

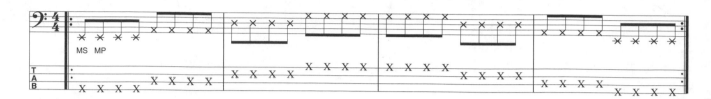

Ex. 22

Ex. 23

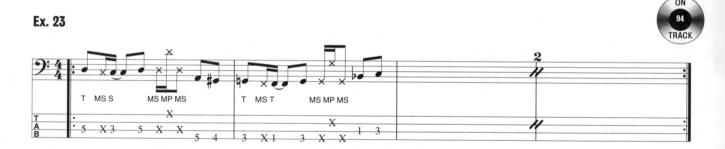

Ex. 24

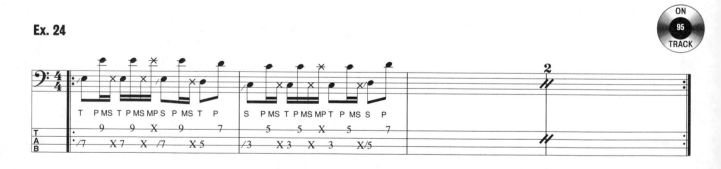

Left-hand slap (LS)

In this technique, you slap the strings with the fretting hand.

Bass riffs using the left-hand slap technique.

Left-hand slap

Ex. 25

ON 96 TRACK

Ex. 26

ON 97 TRACK

Exercises combining all the previous slap-bass techniques

Ex. 27

ON 98 TRACK

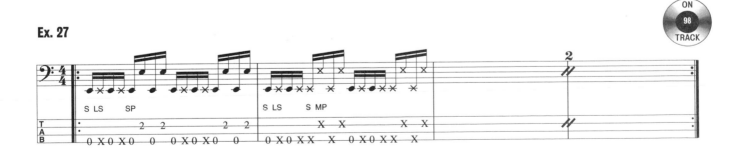

Ex. 28

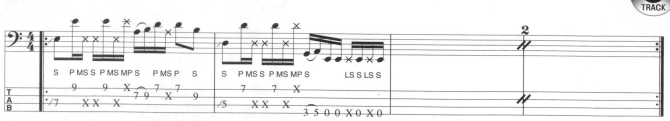

Tapping single notes

Fretboard Tapping

This amazing technique, pioneered on guitar in the mid '70s by Eddie Van Halen, was later adapted to the bass by the likes of Billy Sheehan, Stu Hamm, and Victor Wooten. To perform it, tap (T) onto the fretboard with the plucking-hand index or middle finger, and then pull off (PO) to the note fretted by the other hand. You may also hammer (H) to another note with your fretting hand.

Make sure you listen to the audio on the provided CD to understand the exact feel of these exercises.

Tapping single notes

Ex. 29

Ex. 30

Tapping chords

Tapping chords

ON 102 TRACK

Ex. 31

* Hold down these notes with the fretting hand so that they create a chord sound.

ON 103 TRACK

Ex. 32

* Hold down these notes with the fretting hand so that they create a chord sound.

Section 5
Bass Playing Styles

This section will help broaden the variety of musical styles that you can play. The audio CD's Bass Playing Styles section contains audio excerpts corresponding to all of the Examples in this section. On the CD, the first half of each Example includes the bass line for you to learn. We've repeated the progression or pattern multiple times so you can get a good feel for the bass line. In the second half of each Example, we've omitted the bass line from the audio track. This will allow you to practice playing the bass line you learned in the first half of the Example.

Hip-Hop Bass Lines

Swing Feel

Swing feel refers to a triplet interpretation of eighth-note rhythms. This bouncy feel is contrary to the even eighth-notes of traditional funk, pop, and rock, and closer to jazz and shuffle-style blues. With standard eighth-notes, each beat is equally divided into halves. In swing feel, the first eighth-note of each pair is given two-thirds of a beat, while the second eighth-note receives one-third of a beat.

In swing feel, when you see this:

You play this:

Ex. 1 (swing feel)

Ex. 2 (swing feel)

Ex. 3 (swing feel)

Ex. 4 (swing feel)

Funk Bass Lines

Ex. 5

Ex. 6

Ex. 7

ON
110
TRACK

Ex. 8

ON
111
TRACK

Ex. 9

ON
112
TRACK

Ex. 10

ON
113
TRACK

Old School R&B Bass Lines

Ex. 11

Ex. 12 (swing feel)

Ex. 13

Ex. 14 (swing feel)

Ex. 15

Disco Bass Lines

Ex. 16

Ex. 17

Ex. 18

Ex. 19

Ex. 20

Smooth Jazz Bass Lines

Ex. 21 (swing feel)

ON
124
TRACK

Ex. 22

ON
125
TRACK

Ex. 23

ON
126
TRACK

Ex. 24 (swing feel)

Ex. 25

Ex. 26 (swing feel)

Reggae Bass Lines

Ex. 27

Ex. 28

Ex. 29

Ex. 30 (swing feel)

Ska Bass Lines

Ex. 31

Ex. 32

Latin Bass Lines

Ex. 33

Ex. 34

Ex. 35

Ex. 36

Ex. 37

Ex. 38

World Beat Bass Lines

Ex. 39

Ex. 40

Blues Bass Lines

Ex. 41

Ex. 42

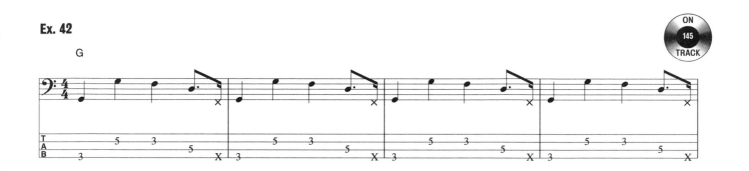

Country Bass Lines

Ex. 43

Ex. 44

Gmaj

Ex. 45

Gmaj

Ex. 46

ON TRACK 149

Gmaj

Rock Bass Lines

Ex. 47

ON TRACK 150

F#m

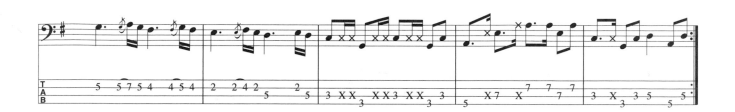

Ex. 48

ON TRACK 151

Em

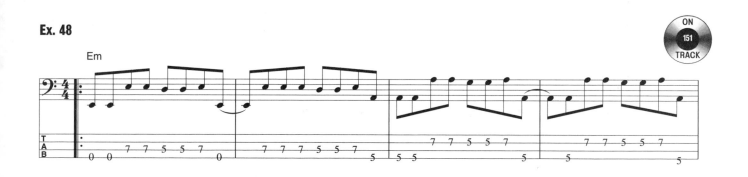

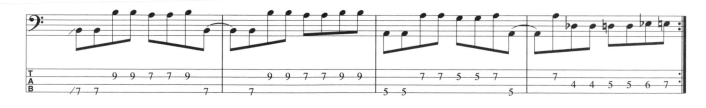

Ex. 49

ON
152
TRACK

G

Ex. 50

ON
153
TRACK

G

Metal Bass Lines

Ex. 51

ON
154
TRACK

Fm

Ex. 52

Ex. 53

Ex. 54

Ex. 55

About the Author

Session bass player, author, producer, and songwriter Josquin des Pres began his career in France in the mid 1970s when he landed his first record deal, signing his fusion band with RCA Records. He has since shared credits with some of the biggest names in the music industry: **Jeff Porcaro**, **Alex Acuña**, **Vinny Colaiuta**, **Jerry Donahue**, **Billy Sheehan**, **Nick D'Virgilio**, **Bunny Brunel**, **Steve Lukather**, **David Garibaldi**, **Jerry Goodman**, **Jimmy Crespo**, **Scott Gorham**, and many others.

In addition to his playing career, Josquin des Pres has authored 14 best-selling bass instructional books and two guitar instructional books. *Old School Funk Bass*, distributed by Big Fish Audio, is a CD-ROM of over 500 of his funkiest bass lines in audio and Acid loop formats. Josquin has also taken an interest in matters pertaining to the music industry and musicians' success within the business. This has led to the writing of two self-help titles for musicians: *Creative Careers in Music* and *Reality Check*.

As a producer and songwriter, Josquin des Pres has produced hundreds of recordings and has had numerous songs covered by international artists. He is one of the very few to collaborate on several songs with **Elton John**'s legendary lyricist, **Bernie Taupin**.

CD Credits & Acknowledgments

The tracks on the included CD are recorded in MP3 format, playable with audio applications such as QuickTime, Windows Media Player, and RealPlayer, or on disc players that read MP3 files.

Bass: **Josquin des Pres**

Drums: **Michael Evans, Enrique Platas**, and **Nick D'Virgilio**

Percussion: **Jay Machan**

Guitar: **Sean Morrissey, Guy Gonzales, David Stark, Mario Olivares, Brett Wiesman**, and **Richie TerBush**

Keyboards: **Carl Evans, Scott Gorham, Sean Morrissey**, and **Neftali Rojas**

Saxophone & flute: **Chris Klich**

Recorded, edited, mixed, and mastered at Track Star Studios, La Mesa, California
Recording engineers: **Sean Morrissey** and **Brett Wiesman**
Editing, mixing, and CD mastering: **Sean Morrissey**

Notation proofing: Phil Dolganov

Photography: **Thom Vollenweider**

Josquin des Pres uses **Carvin** and **Vigier** basses, **Carvin** amps, and **La Bella** strings.

Track Star Studios uses **Nomad Factory** plug-ins and **Tannoy** speakers.

Some of the Latin audio tracks courtesy **Mario Olivares** ("Festival").
Some of the metal audio tracks courtesy **Marlena Randall** ("At Any Hour").
Used by permission.

Special thanks to my kids, Chloé and Julien, for being so patient while I was working on this book late at night; to Nam Chi Vu; and to all the great musicians who played on the audio CD.

Traditional Terms, Signs & Symbols

Repeat terms & signs

D.C. al Fine	Return to the beginning and play to Fine.
D.S. al Fine	Return to 𝄋 and play to Fine.
D.C. al Coda	Return to the beginning, play to ⊕ and skip to the Coda.
D.S. al Coda	Return to 𝄋 , play to ⊕ and skip to the Coda.
𝄇	Return to the beginning or nearest 𝄆 and repeat.

Play through 𝄇 the first time, then skip to ⌐2.⌐ on the repeat.

Symbols

	tenuto	Hold full value
>		Accent
∧	*marcato*	Louder accent
sfz	*sforzando*	Sudden accent
·	*staccato*	Detached
⌢	*fermata*	Hold, pause
<	*crescendo*	Gradually louder
>	*decrescendo diminuendo*	Gradually softer
rit.	*ritardando*	Gradually slower
accel.	*accelerando*	Gradually faster
8va	*All 'ottava*	One octave higher
tr〰〰	trill	Rapid alternation between primary note and note above
♪	grace note	Very short ornamental note (Note: grace notes are always stemmed up)
//	break	Short pause

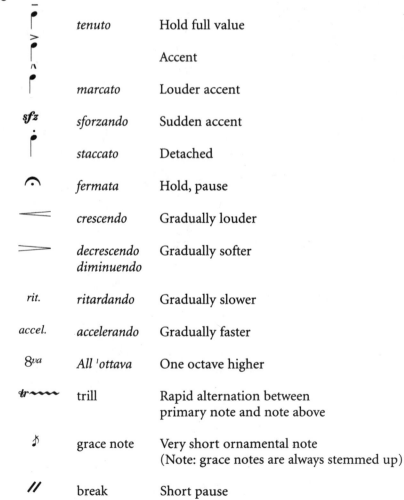

Swing Feel

Swing feel refers to a triplet interpretation of eighth-note rhythms. This bouncy feel is contrary to the even eighth-notes of traditional funk, pop, and rock, and closer to jazz and shuffle-style blues. With standard eighth-notes, each beat is equally divided into halves. In swing feel, the first eighth-note of each pair is given two-thirds of a beat, while the second eighth-note receives one-third of a beat.

In swing feel, when you see this:

You play this: